AF446159

Muskan, Priyanshu & Anushka are the students of standard 10th whose deep, witty and brutally honest thoughts on Thinking, Education & Relationships helped hundreds of people.

In this book they have encapsulated all the experiences of adolescence they face as a teenager. The Rote Learning Education System, The Thinking of the Society and The Relationships & Marriages. This book contains experiences and brutally honest truths about the society. This is not just a book; It is a collection of experiences and real-life stories. This is a book to be read and reread. A book whose line you will underline and think about again and over again.

Something that killed millions of dreams, Something that manipulated millions of thoughts and Something that stops you from chasing your dream and questioning them WHY?

EXPLORING THE DARKER SIDES

UNWRAPPING THE REALITIES

MUSKAN PATHAK

PRIYANSHU SINGH

ANUSHKA KASHYAP

Dedicated to Remind You &
Put Words to Your
Thoughts.

CONTENTS

PREFACE

From daily fights with elders, to arguing for our freedom, from debating about our grades, to getting scolded for keeping our views, from trying to give opinions, to getting ignored by everyone because of our age factor. All of this led us to write this very book, where we won't be interrupted by being called "immature". Where the opinions and views of ours will no longer remain disguised under the covers of the so-called social validation. This book may very well turn out to be the most useless book you will ever buy. Because nothing in this book is something you do not know of. This book is not going to be a revelation or in ferreting out some facts. It is meant to be a reminder.

Criticized by society, ignored by the world, no one ever tried to understand our perspective. After working hard and struggling with our everyday lives, all that we need at the end of the day is peace. But society won't let you live the way you feel comfortable. Did you follow the rules and regulations of our society today? No? Then how come you consider yourself a successful and hardworking person? Weren't you able to score better than your relative's child? Are you a 25-

year-old woman and still not married? How much do you earn? Are you in a relationship or what? Is your husband younger than you? If your answer to any of the questions mentioned above is "yes", then I really feel sorry for you as you weren't able to cope with the conservative standards of our society. But don't worry, you're not alone, we're also the victims of the toxic bullets of judgement that surrounds us whenever we do something unacceptable by our so-called society. Trying to defend ourselves with the shield of confidence, anger and fear at the same time. Fear of losing confidence and getting our anger turned into tears. And once this fear occupies your confidence, you'll be left with nothing but a life which would be no less than the society's puppet. Petrified? Oh, but this was just a glimpse. You'll get a better view of the dark sides of our society once you start reading this book, when the truth will start becoming darker with every flip of the pages.

PART 1
ELDER'S: A MIND WITH EXPERINCES

But, you may say, we asked you to speak about thinking and the generation-gap what, has it got to do with our writing? I will try to explain. I sat down in my room in the moonlight, absorbed with my own thoughts and assumptions about this. Every time I put up a fight in my house, then settle down with guilt and regret about all the shit I made everyone go through. But at last, I am always hoping to find a way and learn morals. My brain starts thinking a lot about where things went wrong and ends up with just one question: who was wrong?

Well, it's not hard to point out the fact that we as "teenagers" differ from our "elders" at every stage of life. But, the hard thing here is to decide who actually is wrong? Either "us" or "our elders". There is a very thin gap between what's right and what's horrible; our differences lie in the middle of this. We differ in almost all subjects in our day-to-day life. We hold different opinions and resonance in most of the subjects; we differ politically, socially, and in almost every such thinking-wise context. How we, being individuals of the same species, fail to understand each other, comfort each other, and most importantly how we fail to work on our differences together instead argue, and then we pretend how civilized our kind is.

(The sudden conglomeration of an idea at the end of one's line; and then the cautions hauling it in, and carefully laying it out? Alas, how insignificant this thought of mine looked) I will not trouble you with any thought now, though if you look carefully you may find it for yourselves in the course of what I am going to say.

However, at any rate, when a subject is highly controversial - one cannot hope to tell the truth

One can only show how one came to hold whatever opinion one does hold. Lies will flow from my lips, but there may be perhaps some truth mixed up with them; it is for you to seek out this truth and to decide whether any part of it is worth keeping. If not, you will of course throw the whole of it into the waste-paper basket and forget all about it. (I give you my thoughts as they came to me)

Well in my belief they open their box of age-old experience and expertise and choose their answers and steps for a better life. Maybe they are never wrong and it's just about the generation gap. Or maybe it's like they never try to see who we really are. It is all about misconceptions and misunderstandings that we have for each other.

Here's a theory about how the parental brain works from my research Parental experience, as well as changing hormone levels during pregnancy and postpartum, cause changes in the parental brain. Displaying maternal sensitivity towards infant cues, processing those cues and being motivated to engage socially with her infant and attend to the infant's needs in any context could

be described as mothering behavior
and is regulated by many systems in
the maternal brain. Research has
shown that hormones such as oxytocin,
prolactin, estradiol and progesterone
are essential for the onset and the
maintenance of maternal behavior in
rats, and other mammals as well.
Mothering behavior has also been
classified as known about the paternal
brain, but changes in the father's brain
occur alongside the mother once the
offspring is born. [Source- Wikipedia]
When anyone becomes a new parent
all they think about is the well-being of
their child. This love and care that they
have for their kids further remolds'
into an emotional behavior of over-
protectiveness and dismal feeling that
everybody around their kids would
harm them. So, here's a fun

thing: next time you are angry about your parents' behavior, excuse them for it (well it's natural, you can't do much about it :)
Parenting is not an easy task, you can put all your energy, time and strength just to make your kids life comfortable and bring him/her all the happiness they deserve according to you.

Well in my point-a-view elders lack the respect that they expect to get throughout their life. They dedicate their lives to fulfilling the dreams of others. They spend most of their lives under the pressure and frame set by society. As humans age they go through a lot of hardships and discomforts in their respective life,

Walter Scott said he that follows the advice of reason has a mind that is elevated above the reach of injury that sits above the clouds in a calm and quiet ether and with a brave Indifference hears the rolling thunders grumble and burst under his feet. The nervousness, pressure, consternation and a lot of bravery accompanied by sacrifice reshape the personality of our elders.

All they want is a better life for their upcoming generation. In order to provide all possible comforts, they refuse to chase their own dreams and start sacrificing their own plans for kids and other responsibilities. They are ready to sacrifice everything they have to make others happy. But yet, such satisfaction comes with a great cost of respect, dignity, and validation they want to get from the society in order to be on their good list. They are ready to put everyone in their relationship just to get validation from others. And at this very moment things start getting worse, differences are laid down to walk on and they are ready to submit anything they have in order to get validation from the society. This game of validation I would further like to explain in my next segment.

Most of the parents buried a lot of their dreams that they dreamt of as children just for the sake of providing a good life to their kids. They don't lose their hopes till the last light in the city is turned off in contemplation to help their kids have a good life.
Here's a story about my own parents.

Like most of the kids I thought my
parents are the best, but as I grew up I
realized yet they are not perfect.
I saw them having a sleepless night
when I caught cold,
I saw the panic in their eyes that they
try to hide before giving me a stern
punishment, life lessons are shared
every day,
Sometimes it is annoying, other times
it shades the light on my dark reality,
I grow with them every day, and
rekindle my thoughts and ideas as
theirs,
Through their stories and inspiration, I
heard growing up.
Sometimes I'm happy to be their part
to have their thoughts and ideas,
Sometimes I feel like being stuck
around their box of ideology,

I want to see the world through their
eyes and expertise,
I hate, that I can't voice my own
opinions,
I wish I could understand them,
I wish they could try to know how my
world works.
Well, when I look deep down inside
their dark brown eyes all I see is love
and affection for me, suppressed under
the worthless game of validation.

Well, I don't know much about how
one's mind works and how it changes
as we get older. One may lose their
patience and calmness while waiting
for the growth of the sweet fruit, they
put all the energy and resources they
ever had. So, they are way too tired by
the end to hear the miseries and
mishaps we had in our lives. They

already invested all they had, and when they see us fall it hurts them. But stern measures are necessary for our betterment. They are raised under very strict conditions. They try to teach us all the life lessons they had, they want us to grow up as a better version of them and learn from their past mistakes. My dad would always compare his young days with mine, he would say-'you are brat because we have provided you with all the lavishness (right after providing me with the very basic belonging that is required for my every day life), in our times we used to walk 10000 miles every day for our school. So it's like they want us to always know the ground reality. It's a very different sort of relation we share with our parents;

we have the best love-hate-love
relation.

They realized when they are wrong;
they love us a lot more than they love
anything else in this materialistic
world. They would never show us even
the little glimpse of change they had
because of us. Every day they might
wake up with a thought of being better
for no one else, but us, to be there for
no matter how wrong things went
down, no matter what crimes we
committed. They would stick around
us through thick and thin. I don't know
if this helps, I don't know if I have
explained sufficient things about our
elders but this is all I could think and
explain about.

PART 2
TEENAGER'S: A MESSY MIND.

*One moment we're
broken,
And then we're fine,
It's all one puzzle,
Inside teenager's mind
[Tate McRae]*

Well, I guess these lines better explain
us rather than my words. It's like a
very big beautiful mess that you enjoy
but regrets at the same time.
It is beautiful and traumatizing at the
same time. It is like a loop- you fall;
you get up, and fall again. When you
experience everything for the very first
time, you feel like an adult without
being one. It remains a strange and

almost inexplicable life period where we commit beautiful crimes, confess pretty lies and go through a very emotional merry-go-round. Sometimes it feels like how good life seemed, how sweet its reward, how trivial this grudge or that grievance, how admirable friendship and the society of one's kind.

These years are filled with a personal roller coaster; we've to make very difficult personal choices on various matters. We have to make big decisions about life, education, career, love, and various other affairs. We are afraid to take guidance, seek feedback and make our own decisions through other's past experiences and choices. We have trust issues in every moment of our life and trusting our intuitions can barely land us somewhere safe and sound. These decisions are not just about right or wrong, but also about our own capacity to implement it and face the outcome. So here we don't have the patience to listen to anyone's age-old experience and expertise. We go through various emotional and physical hormonal changes that make us intolerant and incapable of listening. Puberty can be a very difficult time for children. They're coping with changes in their body, at a time when they feel very self-conscious and self- doubt fills up their young minds. Puberty is a very exhilarating time, as children develop new emotions and feelings. But the "emotional rollercoaster" they're on can have psychological and emotional effects, such as:

- Unexplained mood swings

- Low self-esteem
- Aggression
- Depression

We are unsure in ourselves about what's wrong with our minds. The constant change in our behavior is mainly due to the lack of acceptance we get around ourselves. We don't get comfort in school as well as in our homes. We are under the constant pressure of pushing off our limits that we set on our own. Suggestions and constant nagging from everyone around us push us away from our own closed ones. Seriously, however, if we could learn enough about our physical life and emotional changes in the aging and change of our body we could have done things better off. Our irritation and anger are not just alone because of the hormonal changes our body and mind go through, but a wide percentage of this is because of other's behavior of constant poking and pressure. And that when elders start thinking we are grown up and stop giving attention to our mental and social well-being but rather start focusing on more materialistic things. An old notebook of mine lay beside me and, opening it, I turned casually enough to a random blank page where I've scribbled something in the bottom-most corner in anger and agitation. The words are scribbled with gel pens that are smudged due to the various droplets of tears that left its imprint on the page. It was shouting emotions of a young me in less but very clear words, it goes like;

In home town,
I'm a bird in a cage,
Loved but not allowed to
fly,
I want to learn how to use
my wings,
I think I've the calibre to
conquer the world.

There was something so ludicrous in thinking about my mental state at this time. I feel most kids my age feel the same way. Yet we all are strangers, lacking the same things or going through the same emotions but we can't comfort one another during such times. We feel like being judged most of the time, by almost everybody. That's another reason why we can't confess our thoughts and minds all the time in front of our own family. The relentless thoughts we have before bringing ourselves to talk. We get confused between our own thoughts and illusions. "Quiet down I begged my mind, your over thinking is robbing us of joy" [Rupi Kaur]

All was going well before it wasn't. There was excitement and elation before there wasn't. That's the thing about fantasy and reality. In your own la la land, you can be a mediator of superpowers or imagine yourself stopping a big clash between two giant parties, that's how we teenagers live our life. We create some sort of uncomfortable world in our minds that

is not much different from our reality
and tends to live that way. Acceptance
that we lack in our surroundings, the
knowledge about basic life that is not
taught to us makes things worse for us.
We are provided with little to no
knowledge about what sort of changes
are going to take place inside our
bodies. No one shares how to tackle
the emotional roller coaster that we are
about to ride. Most kids are lucky
enough to go school (a place where
one expects to learn almost everything
necessary) in this time period but these
educational premises do not provide us
with basic life living skills and the
necessary knowledge that one should
know before entering this phase. No
one talks about our body, mind, sexual
well-being and other necessary things
that one should know.

I would like to share my own
experience from this time period.
(Won't call it my age-old experience).
Well keeping aside all science stuff -I
believe I started considering myself a
full grown-up teen for the first time
when I had my first menstruation flow.
It was a complete trauma for someone
like me who believes going through
puberty as a young girl is so confusing.
This monster invades your body,
changes things and makes things grow,
and no one tells you what's going on.
(Still, I consider myself lucky to have
at least basic knowledge about it.)
I remember that day very vividly.
It was late March, the sun's radiance
burning my skin while I played
carelessly with my friends.

Tired and young me went back home
with great energy to tell everyone the
story of my triumph.
But suddenly all my energy vanished
away.
I felt a rush of uneasiness and pain
flowing through every vein of my
body.
Well, when I checked it was blood that
stuck around my body and the fear
took the place of energy in my mind
and soul.
I cried for I don't know how long
before I was ready to tell my mom that
I guess I'm an adult like you now.
I saw a soft smile in her eye and
concern in her voice before she gave
me a pad to apply.
For the rest of the night, I pressed my
face deep in the pillow ignoring the

beautiful moon impression that fell on the mirror.

A long trail of tears fell from my eyes that had more questions than answers anyone ever had.

To question the universe something seemed lacking, something seemed different. But what was lacking, what was different, I asked myself, listening to my grief.

I still think it was beautiful when I was younger.

The next day, I went to school with a very different agitation to tell my girlfriends I am grown up like them now.

I think it was strange as I was already tamed to not tell my male friend anything about my pain, anger and irritation. They looked at me with astonishment, unable to ask the weird question that aroused in their mind; I still can see it in their desperate eyes. Well, I still don't understand why we are tamed this way. Why does everyone think it's ok to be quiet when it simply is not ok? The research shows that;

Out of 600, 245 (40%) girls remained absent from school during their menstruation. School absenteeism was significantly associated with the type of absorbent used, lack of privacy at school, restrictions imposed on girls during menstruation, mother's education, and source of information on menstruation. Nearly 65% reported that it affected their daily activities at school and that they had to miss their class tests and classes as a result of pain, anxiety, shame, anxiety about leakage, and staining of their uniform.

Here's a stats to get your blood boiling: 42% of US women say they have experienced period-shaming by men and nearly 60% of women feel embarrassed when they menstruate, due in large part to pervasive taboos and the attitudes of men. The toxic culture of taming girls to not share anything about their periods in school is still widely practiced. The weird culture of connecting periods with pride and shame or somewhat dignity of a girl is tagged with her throughout her life.
Well, I think it's all about lack of education and fault in our society which we will discuss in the next segment.

I've made a lot of mistakes during this period. Made a lot of wrong choices,

put up various unnecessary fights.
There are various occasions where I
was absurdly wrong but my new
teenage brain did not know how to
stop putting up unnecessary fights.
I think I enjoy my teen years. It's good
and bad; it's poor and rich, happy and
sad, cool and quiet. I think it's simply
too confusing and hard to give a tag. I
fear my best years are behind me and
nothing beyond this point will add up.
You know the only thing, anyone, as a
teenager regret is, falling relationship
with their parents. We don't want to
hurt them but, when sometimes no one
in the world understands us, we expect
some support from our parents. We
still love our parents as we used to
when we were young kids, but there's a
lot of things running in our minds. We
can't manage everything, in order to

manage everything, we fail in most of the things.

Exposure to the outside world is very necessary for all teenagers. Having the direct mindset or beliefs of parents doesn't help in a long race. Having a combination of mindset from our parents as well as lessons from the outside world works for almost every individual.

Parents should start trusting their children at some point, they should show their faith and trust in us. Sometimes hiding your feelings for each doesn't help, things take a very wrong turn. We still have time to look for mistakes on our part and start rebuilding.

We would get better and come stronger, don't lose hope. We are still your kids, wouldn't be that wrong.

PART 3
THINKING DIFFRENCES &
GENERATION GAP

Now let's start discussing where our differences lie.

Generation gap: it stands for the difference in values and attitudes between one generation and another, especially between younger people and their parents. The difference results in greater misunderstandings where both are not ready to perceive feelings, habits and lifestyles of each other toward one's life. I agree we as humans do not tend to have the same or even similar opinions on any matter. We can't expect anyone to hold the same ideology as another individual in any matter about life or other such general terms. We all know this and this is the only matter we can agree on. Yet, nobody is ready to respect the idea of another individual. It's not just about teenagers holding their ideas against elders and mockingly making fun of it, such things are done by both parties. We don't have the tendency to hear the ideas of one another without anger or without planning to put up a fight for our ideology. And that's what our relationships lack and differences take shelter in our homes without invitation.

The basic differences are regarding how society operates. And I believe there are a lot of loopholes in this subject. We belong to different eras and the fact is we lack these basic life skills of giving chance to another individual. Nobody is ready to accept the slightest change in their lives. We live in a world where it is easy to accept the wrong system then simply raise a voice against it. We are so used to the fake image before the society that we are ready to sacrifice all our as well as our close one's happiness for it. The idea of acceptance from society is so necessary that we can't afford the idea of accepting our own flaws. This idea of not accepting our own mistakes leads to a life of very high ego regarding the simplest achievements as well as assets of our life. We not only clash for our difference's generation-wise, but we put up scenes as we simply do not want to accept someone else's idea in regard to our own betterment. No one wants to stand up against the wrong mindset of people in this so-called society, and if somebody raises their voice, they are considered a victim of modernization and are stopped from raising their voices.

And that's where the main clash between the millennial and boomers vs. gen-z starts.

PART 4
MEN, WOMEN &
PATRIARCY

The first matter that I would like to pick in the context of the difference is misogyny and patriarchy. Most people believe feminism stands for the equality of women and such definition comes out from very misogynistic mouths itself. The idea of feminism standing just for women's rights arises mainly due to the word being taken for its literal meaning. On the contrary, feminism stands for the right of every individual irrespective of their caste, class, gender and sexuality. No matter where you come from, what your educational and economical status is, you as an individual deserve equal opportunities in every possible field of human interest. No one, I repeat no one can take away your basic rights and ideas you have about your own life. And most of the millennial and boomers are not ready to accept this small fact. We are living in the 21st century, still not being able to accept this for the fact that everyone deserves equal rights and opportunities just to show how are we willing to ruin our lives with such inadequate thinking. The first one to suffer in the process of such a backward mindset of misogyny and patriarchy is the women's. Patriarchy is sexual colonization in which gender relationships are in terms of domination and subordination. This ingenious form of internal colonization results in the human and undignified treatment

Of women. Men develop a utilitarian attitude to women and expect

Total and unconditional servility from them.

Women at a very young age are taught that they have to grow up to raise a family; our sole responsibility of being female is to devote our lives for the sake of our husbands and children. We are always taught to be too polite, too kind, and too sweet towards everything we face including all the discomforts. We are always asked to stay easy, change however and whenever according to the situation. It's hard being a woman when you are circled by people with a very sick mindset. While growing up as a female I have seen everybody providing me with very odd and sexist opinions every now and then. I would dress according to others preferences, express my views according to others' opinions, and do basically everything according to others choices. Women are not

believed to have a mind of their own, they should always rule under the guidance of some male character in her life. She can't leave home alone, she can't do this, and she shouldn't do that. I saw these very beautiful yet honest lines from one of Kamala Das's poems, it says: -" We have no hand or voice in the management of our social affairs. In India, man is lord and master. He has taken to himself all powers and privileges
And shut up the women in the zenana." Subordination is something that is expected by women from a very young age. We are taught how to submit ourselves not just to our would-be-husbands, but literally to every member of his family. It is a whole set of ideas that had been practiced for many years. The Wife is expected to

have her views and ideas in favour of their husbands, they are considered to be the chief head of the family. The Husband's decision will always overrule the decision of the wife. In matters of financial terms husbands, the opinion would prevail as they are the bread earners of the family. Women's choices are always suppressed under the supremacy of their male partners. Soon or later, they lose their faith in having an individual opinion and rather start living a life under the shadow of their husband. These circumstances force women to fall under the trap of self-doubt and interdependence on their partners. This could be the main reason why women's individual personality usually covers under pressure and nervousness; they start living their lives more like an object rather than living beings. Such circumstances give rise to thoughts like: -

"Dying

Is an art, like everything else.

I do it exceptionally well." (Kamala Das)

They lose their individuality and forget themselves completely; such incidents give rise to a woman who has no dreams about herself in her life. Rather she surrenders herself to her husband.

I see patriarchy spoiling the lives of almost every man. They become a victim of societal pressures. They are often asked to "man up" and forced to do more physical as well as financial services than their partners. Men have to go through a lot of emotional ups and downs but, they are not expected to show their emotions as it would make them less, mainly they say. The idea of man being masculine, aggressive and violent is forced into the minds of very young kids. They are never actually provided with emotional care, they are often the victims of ignorance and over-pressure, for financial support. If a crime of rape or any other sexual offences are reported by men, the society is not ready to believe it. The ignorance and cold-heartedness towards their misery provoke men to further hide their fear and insecurities within a hard nutshell of aggression. This society questions the masculinity of a man too often.

*The son of the patriarchal father the
mantle of dad he does don
And in his sons and their sons
patriarchy will live on
And though the praises of patriarchy
many may sing
What it stands for to say the least is
not a good thing
In patriarchal societies war is
glorified
As well as love of Flag of Country
and National pride
Such things that to war always does
seem to lead
Of peace loving people we seldom do
hear of or read*

*Far too many patriarchal societies in
the World of today
We'd be better off without them is all
I can say
Far too many patriarchs in every
town
Who glorify war and keep women
down
Patriarchs are not rare they do live
everywhere
There are millions of them in the big
World out there.* (Francis Duggan)

Patriarchy is wrecking our whole system. It will barely take a few more years before this whole system of putting/pushing women would collapse the whole society.

This evil mindset of people is somewhat not limited to uncivilized households but almost everywhere around the world one can face this thing, or basically become an innocent victim of such a very dangerous societal flaw.

PART 5
Women and Misogyny

I see women being the victim of hatred, prejudice, injustice and crime. I see women taking up the blame for everything happening around them. I think the main reason behind this mindset is, ever since childhood, we are taught how to take blame for everything. We are taught how not to live a life with dignity and self-esteem. Women are questioned most of the time for anything wrong conceivably happening with them. This cruel mindset of society forces women to withdraw various decisions of their own lives and re-shape them according to the parameters set by our so-called society, whose validation is somewhat much more important than covid-19 vaccinations.

Everyone tells you how women should live, but no one accepts women living by themselves, however, she feels like. The basic set of rules that are required by any individual is also messed up so that women don't get the freedom that is necessary for their own livelihood. From Very young age, women are asked to take up the responsibility (the word used by society) of each and every man around them. If you start questioning the very normal (something that is not normal, but we are expected to normalize) day-to-day things you would easily plot how wrongly our society is functioning. It's always the female member of the family, to cook, to serve, to clean, and to please and never the male. Your younger/elder brothers are not expected to have the same involvement in household affairs as you. This internalized misogyny leads to bigger sexism events in the future.

I have seen elders coming in, sitting in my house and discussing things about my life, which is absolutely none of their business. They would ask questions about my cooking and cleaning skills. If they are given a brutally honest answer, they would weep their eyes in shame, now who will marry this very problematic mam. Sexism is normalized almost everywhere around the world. In schools, in houses, on the street, in airports. Like, literally everywhere people are okay with the very sexist point. When questions are asked, they would simply answer, it's something society has accepted. Me and you can simply not change. The fact that sexism is normalized to the extent, that

these small-small things give rise to
the very prominent "rape culture " of
our high class(infamous) society,
whose validation is more important
than having a regular health check-up.
Often this ignored patriarchy gives rise
to a path of misogyny that consists of
greater sexism, providing blind support
to the rape culture.

Rape Culture

Rape culture is something,
In which rape is pervasive and
normalized due to societal attitudes
about gender and sexuality.
Behaviours commonly associated with
rape culture include victim-blaming,
slut-shaming, sexual objectification,

trivializing rape, and denial of widespread rape, refusing to acknowledge the harm caused by sexual violence or some combination of these. It has been used to describe and explain behaviour within social groups, including prison rape and in conflict areas where war rape is used as psychological warfare. Entire societies have been alleged to be rape cultures. It is associated with rape fantasy and rape pornography.

Victim blaming

The idea any women could be raped was a new proposition that called attention to the notion of victim-blaming. Now that rape could affect anyone, there would not be a proper way for men and women to avoid it. Some rape myths that were widely accepted based on of what kind of women would be raped were ideas that the victim was always "young, careless [and] beautiful" or they are "loose" women who "invite rape" by provoking men." Although Brown miller's idea about victim blaming was supposed to expose rape myths thus eradicating victim-blaming, blaming the victim in rape circumstances is still a common practice.

Victim-blaming may also occur among a victim's peers, and college students have reported being ostracized if they report a rape against them, particularly if the alleged perpetrator is a popular figure or noted athlete. Also, while there is generally not much general discussion of rape facilitated in the home, schools, or government agencies, [where?] such conversations may perpetuate rape culture by focusing on techniques of "how not to be raped" (as if it were provoked), vs "how not to rape." This is problematic due to the stigma created and transgressed against the already victimized individuals rather than stigmatizing the aggressive actions of rape and the rapists. It is also commonly [specify] viewed that prisoners in prison deserve to be raped and is a reasonable form of punishment for the crimes they committed. [better source needed] Another factor of victim-blaming involves racism and racial stereotypes. Victim-blaming has serious consequences as it helps further perpetuate pervasive rape-culture. Victims who receive negative responses when disclosing sexual violence tend to experience greater distress and are therefore less likely to report future incidents if they occur.

Slut shaming

Slut shaming may be considered similar to victim blaming in that there is a condemnation of someone who has been involved in a sexual event or event. The key difference is that victim-blaming involves the person being condemned for being a victim who has provoked their attacker (e.g., because they wore more revealing clothing, they are condemned for being coerced or physically forced into being involved in a sexual event), and slut shaming is based upon the person being condemned for their willing participation in a sexual event. Slut shaming describes the way people are made to feel guilty or inferior for certain sexual behaviours or desires that deviate from traditional or orthodox gender expectations. A study of college women from sociologists at the University of Michigan and the University of California found that slut-shaming had more to do with a woman's social class than it did with their activity. Slut-shaming can create a double standard between men and women and discrimination.

One thing is very clear that for the record it will always be a woman to blame. These double standards of society change their definitions time-to-time in order to throw the blame on women.

Women are taught to be mum or stay quiet about every injustice she has to face. Often her life/protection is regarded as the pride of the family. So, she is not provided with equal treatment when any such injustice happens to her. She could not expect her own family members to support her during such circumstances.

This is something I had in my mind forever, before going out I would question my outfit, my makeup and everything. This constant thought of not putting up something too revealing, too extra, not wearing too much makeup would make me question myself. The fact that since childhood, I feel like it would be my fault if I would wear something extra and go out. I have always taken the blame on myself. All the cat callings, comments, uncomfortable touches in public, I took the blame on myself. Well, it was just standard 8th when I realized no matter what I wear, I would face this in public. There are various events in my life when I was scared to go out, even in the sunny daylight. But, don't you think I have an equal right on the beautiful crescent moon? Why should I sacrifice my young days, just because there is someone else with an upset mindset? I've heard it quite often, don't go out alone, go with papa or bhaiya, but on the contrary, I've been cat-called in their presence. To everyone's surprise, they also decided to stay mum. It's not something that happens to only pretty girls, too skinny girls, when you are wearing something too revealing, too short, and too deep. It happens with anyone, anywhere, anytime.

It literally boils my blood thinking about why it is hard to provide women with the same set of respect that is provided to every Male. Women are not even provided with the basic set of respect even by their own family members. Everything and at every point of time women are deprived of the basic set of rights provided to any human being. It's always the male character who gets more opportunity, responsibility, credits, and financial prowess than a woman. One can question a female's ability any time over a man, but even the smartest female brains are not believed in the very first place. This system of patriarchy accompanied by misogyny is only breaking down the confidence, power, ability to just satisfy their own double standards and divide the world through discrimination and hatred. This system is not doing/providing good to anyone, people need to learn how their ignorance is making someone's life miserable.

Females are living a life of misery and suppression. Not given equal opportunities in any field, the cage of operation is discouraging their brilliant minds. Our ignorance, discomforts, discrimination is the reason we have lost so many brilliant minds that could do wonderful things. All we as women sometimes feel like to: -

*"I shall someday leave,
leave the cocoon
You built around me
with morning tea,
Love-words flung from
doorways and of course
Your tired lust, I shall
someday take
Wings fly around"*
(Kamala das)

Women have ideas and minds of their own. People often overlook their smart minds for the sake of their external bodies.

She lives in you and me and in many other women who are not here tonight and cannot read or write for they are washing up the dishes and putting the children to bed. But she lives; for great humans do not die; they are continuing presences; they only need the opportunity to walk among us in the flesh. This opportunity, as I think, is now coming within our power to give her. If we have the habit of freedom and the courage Express what we think; if we escape a little from the common sitting-room and see human beings not always in their relation to each other but in the relation to the reality; and the sky, two, I'm the trees or whatever it may be in themselves; if we look past our own greed, for no human being should shut out the view, if we face the fact, for it is a fact, that we don't provide everyone with equal opportunities. It's still not too late to point out the flaws and make this world a better place for living.

A lot of fearless women are continuing their presence under violence, abuse, hate, prejudice, slut shaming, and rape culture. A lot are spending their lives in the threat of getting abused anytime. I would like to take a moment and thank every woman for showing courage, for breaking down the stereotypes, for fighting the worst humanitarian crimes, for standing brave in front of the situation, for giving birth to a child, for going

through labour for us. Thank you for
your presence.

PART 6
MENTAL WELL BEING:
CONSIDERATION WITH SHAME

Now,

In this segment I would like to explain our differences regarding mental struggle.

Mental health is a state of well-being in which an individual realizes his or her own abilities, can cope with the normal stresses of life, can work productively and is able to make a contribution to his or her community. Mental health is fundamental to our collective and individual ability as humans to think, emote, interact with each other, earn a living and enjoy life. On this basis, the promotion, protection and restoration of mental health can be regarded as a vital concern of individuals, communities and societies throughout the world. Knowledge of what to do about the escalating burden of mental disorders has improved substantially over the past decade.

The fact that nobody actually prefers talking about any of these issues. There's a lot of stigma attached to our mental illness. Every 1 in 5 adults suffer from a serious mental disorder. Every 1 in 20 teenager's suffers from a mental disorder. And we still are not ready to talk about it openly. We still criticize people for being outspoken for such topics, people would come up with thoughts like, oh! She's exaggerating; it's not a big deal. People instead of providing others with emotional support, ready to tear each other down for their insecurities or discomforts. It's time the world acts as a family and starts supporting each other in such situations. There's absolutely no knowledge provided to anyone about their own mental health. It is lacking to the extent that most people living in rural households of Middle East Asia and south Asia won't realize if they are suffering from mental conditions. Lack of education in this field can be very dangerous to an Individual as well as to the community

People suffer a lot during such hard times, the thought of killing, running away, self-harm is constantly running inside one's brain. Sometimes you don't even realize why you feel this way. It's not even important to have a certain reason to feel like this. No reason is small or big, your problem is big, you have to be strong enough to deal with it. The taboo attached with someone suffering from such things makes it even harder for the person to look up for a solution. Sharing this problem is not an easy task, looking up for professional help is neither easy. The society we live in won't show any acceptance to the person suffering. We need to show people hope in living, beauty in loving themselves. Instead of disrespecting each other for something this serious.

Well, I believe most elders think our depression is a trend, we struggle because of socialization via the internet and spending more time on the phone. Mental illness is taken way too lightly by almost everybody, they think we do this or behave in a particular manner just in order to become "cool". On the other hand, nobody really tries to see our struggle and the need for proper attention for our mental condition. Mental illness is somewhat considered a symbol of weakness. We live in the 21st century with our mindsets still underdeveloped like living in the ice age. The fault of not being mentally well is directly blamed on either our social circle or phones. It's something I believe almost everyone is suffering from at one point of their life. Proper care and support could make things a hundred times better. We really need to understand the seriousness of this condition.

One day while going through an article about suicide, I saw these very beautiful lines written by him before committing such a harsh step.

Before committing suicide, this person scribbled his note book with the following words. I will read a few lines from it, explaining his state of mind:

O sea, I am fed up
I want to be simple
I want to be loved
And
If love is not to be had,
I want to be dead,

Nobody is ready to accept this harsh step; people easily start calling anybody committing suicide as a coward. But, no one is ready to accept their own mistakes in this process. We don't ask questions to ourselves; we still ignore the fact that it is very possible for someone living closed to us can take the same steps.

It's time we start normalizing mental health issues. We stop the taboo of not reaching out for help. Proper medical treatment should be provided to anyone suffering from such issues, irrespect of their ages

It's time we show strength in living, loving and accepting. It's time we support each other no matter what. It's time we show gratitude towards each other.
It's time we break the stereotypes about mental health and talk and share about it as much as possible. Our help, support can save someone's life.

PART 7
EMPTY ROOM:
(1) BUILD FOR DIFFRENCES, BY US.
(2) BEAUTY OF ACCEPTANCE.

Here are some places where I feel we
have great differences: -
We believe in equality, they don't
We believe in right to one's own mind
and choices, they don't
We believe in providing some
individual space (it helps in the better
thinking capacity of our brain), they
don't,
We believe in the existence of
depression, they don't,
We believe in respecting each other's
idea and views, they don't,
We believe in individual decisions of
choosing our sexuality, they don't
They believe in peace, we don't
They believe in experience, we don't
They believe in society, we don't
They believe in us, we don't.
Its time for us to open our eyes and
start looking inside ourselves to stop

breaking away from our owns. Its time we realize our individual mistake and start forgetting each other. There are a lot of differences we have with our parents. I might not be able to bring light on every topic or thoughts that you might have. But, one thing that causes the most damage to our relationship is the basic lack of "communication" within us. When our ideas start to differ, conflicts arise, ideals/ inspiration changes, mindset stops matching. We instead of looking for a way out start ignoring or forcing our ideas on each other. The room for discussions is shut forever, leaving behind the beautiful ruins of our relationship. That's the time when a giant wall of differences is built between us and we start cutting off.

There should be a room for discussions
There should be a room where we hear
each other and understand each other.
There should be a room of no
dominance.
There should be a room where one feel
free and can express oneself in front of
each other.
There should be a room of freedom,
mental break-downs, love and care.
There should be a room where respect
is not given just for the sake of
relationship,
There should be a room of realization,
There should be a room where things
are not done to satisfy society.
There should be room for mistakes,
There should be a room for correction,
There should be a room for a life
without fear and pressure,

There should be a room where
escaping from reality is not needed,
There should be a room for questions
or objections,
There should be a room for answers.
There should be a room for
acceptance.

It's time, when we start looking for
flaws inside us rather than searching
for it in someone else. We as whole
can work together on this and make
our relationships more healthier with
our closed ones. It's not the fault of an
individual, we lack this patience,
compassion and respect for each other
together. It's time we start looking
inside ourselves, and ask what was my
fault?
Where did I go wrong?

How can I explain it to them in a better way?
How should we work on this?
Was everything they shared wrong?
What was the reason behind this?
Why is it hard to accept each other's ideas?
It is not our differences that divide us. It is our inability to accept, recognize and celebrate those differences. If we open our minds and start accepting each other, however hard it seems. Maybe the room of differences can shut down and we can use the empty space to reconstruct our relationship. We as individuals should learn the value of acceptance and should show patience towards others values.

PART 1
EDUCATION SYSTEM

The Indian Education System, where we are studying for marks in lieu of studying for knowledge and so, it SUCKS. The date dates back to 5000 BC or the Vedic age, where all the people including the sons of the king studied under one roof. All were considered equal at the Gurukul. Gurukuls originally emphasised on discipline, humanity, love and brotherhood, but all this disappeared as the modern system of education was brought to India by Lord Macauley in the year 1835. The Modern Education System is job oriented; we merely know to get a degree and go into a company like a servant and we really have no slot here for skill, creativity and talent. There is a complete absence of personality development, creation of moral conscience and ethical training. The modern education system is more commercial in nature rather than an institutional concept which should provide holistic education (The present-day education mainly focuses on a rank-based system which is driven by animosity towards their peers) to the students.

A student commits sucide in India every hour, 12% of Indian students between the age of 4 and 16 suffer from psychiatric disorders, 20% show the signs of mental disorders. More than 1.5 lakh Indian students died by suicide.

My question is - "if we really have such a good mindset, equality, psychological comfort and amazing teachers…"
Then,

- **Why are the students committing suicide?**

- **Why is the nature of this education system so competitive that our students have to commit succeed?**

- **Why are WE creating such a situation that a**

student has to take such a big step?

Believe it or not, since childhood, we have been conditioning that child that passing the exam means success and failing in the exam means failing in life.
After failing an exam, that poor kid thinks that he/she has failed in life because we have glorified people based on their rank.
We have a mindset that a science student is a GENIUS one and a Arts or commerce student is an AVERAGE. In such a situation, we are solely putting pressure on that student.

- Why can't we remove all these rank-based systems?

- Why can't we make education FREE for all?

- Why is there so much competition to get into an educational institution?

To be brutally honest, Our Education System is dud and outdated.

Let's take a practically possible example - We basically have two types of students in a classroom (a place where everyone poses different ambitions and determinations) i.e. The First Benchers & The Last Benchers.

- **The First Benchers**, the ones who are always perceived as optimistic and astute students. They run behind the good grades and spurious happiness and they are the ones who can do their tasks perfectly.

- **The Last Benchers**, the ones who generally sit at the last bench of the classroom by themselves.

They generally do not care about their studies and do very bad things. They shout in the class, fight in the class, bunk the class, etc. In a nutshell, they have a problem with authority but they can do wonders if they are determined.

We know that no one is better, every student has been endowed or blessed with different abilities, talents and capabilities. We differ from each other in the sense that we have different interests and inclinations. One might be good at music but not at drawing, while another might be great at dancing but not at writing.

Students start discovering themselves after standard 8th, So at least some of the subjects should be optimal. However, if every child is different then why are they evaluating each individual in the same way?

. **Why don't we have an aptitude test?**

As Albert Einstein said –

"Everybody is a Genius. But If You Judge a Fish by Its Ability to Climb a Tree, It Will Live Its Whole Life Believing that It is Stupid"

Imagine for a moment with integrity
and probity, who really deserves
this Indian Education System or
what kind of people is this system
dedicated to?

- **Is this education system
  really meant to make
  learning interactive?**

- **Is this education system
  really *meant* that students
  should have a fun-to-learn?**

- **Is this education system
  really meant to make
  lectures interesting,**

something practical or something creative?

No, RIGHT!
Our Indian Education System
wants us to mug up theories rather
than focusing on parting knowledge
through conducting experiments.
They are more focused on making
us mug up the books.

PART 2
INDIAN SOCIETY & MENTALITY AND MODERN-DAY EDUCATION SYSYTEM

The Modern-Day Education
System be like - "Hey, these are
the books for your esteemed class,
LEARN IT THOROUGHLY.
Wait….
Don't you like it?
Never mind, we don't care, give it a
good clean, Mug it up well."

Whatever, but why do we need to
mug up things?
Look, here you need to mug up to
write well in the exam.
This will fetch you good marks in
the exams.
With good marks, you will be able
to get into your favourite college.
Again, this will help you continue
this cycle for the next 4 to 5 years
in your respected college,

which will probably get you a 9 to 5 job,
You will gain money from the job,
And money will make you successful.
That is it, Go Mug up Write, Go Mug up Write, Go Mug up Write.

- **Kill your talent**
- **Kill your creativity**
- **Kill your interest**

And if you feel like this Indian Society and Mentality encourages you to be a good human by their philosophies such as: -

- Study More, that will help you to get a good salaried job.
- Which will help you to improve your living and lifestyle.
- And of course, then you will surely become a good person.

Ah! let's Evaluate this

- An IAS Aspirant writes an essay of 4-5 pages on dowry, which will again help him score well in the exam, then he will become an IAS officer and then he will be the one who is going to take a higher dowry. This is your mentality, Right!

- Most of these 21st-century Indian kids would have proudly put a sticker of 'Dads Gifted' on their car, if their father would have gifted them a car but on the other hand, if they got it as a dowry, they would be very ashamed to put a sticker of 'father-in-law's favour'. This is your society, Right!

- Your family forces you to get a government job not because they care for it but just to bring

that free car, Washing
Machine, Fridge and New
Utensils.

This is how you become a good
human being, Right?
Even if this system were to improve
in the future, it would have already
destroyed millions of dreams.
Did you know that India is the only
country that produces every year
as many engineers as the entire
population of Switzerland?
But still lacks in infrastructural
development, research and
innovation

Our education system, the rote learning-based, mugging up based education system that focuses on theoretical knowledge and taught us: -

- **Learn to mug up**
- **Learn to take orders**
- **Don't ask questions**

This modern-day education system totally destroyed our: -

- **Leadership Quality**
- **Critical Thinking**
- **Decision Making**

There exists a majority of students who don't want to go with physics, chemistry & maths but still ends up becoming an engineer in spite of wanting to go with arts or commerce because our society and their parents force them to take science as our society does not give importance to arts. This Indian Society has developed a mindset that no field is good except PCM or PCB. If you look at my Facebook page, you will see a quote there -

"Degree Doesn't Define The Capability Of A Person, A Person's Capability Can Change The World Without The Degree"

Everyone is taught the same syllabus and the same thing, without looking at their capabilities. *Parting knowledge via experiments and field groups should be enhanced now* else our students will not be able excel in their field even if they are interested.

PART 3

HIERARCHICALSYSTEM, REALITY (AND SUCCESS)

*See, most of our students
choose their stream based on
whether it is difficult or easy.
Nothing is hard or easy, we
have characterised them on
the basis of easy or difficult.
Look it is simple, if you think
that you are an average or
weak student and keeping that
in mind, if you are choosing
your stream then there is no
guarantee that you are going to
excel in your field and this
brings us to the conclusion that
an actual smart student can
excel in any field.*

There is a hierarchical system that exists in this world. One has to work as a barber or a sweeper or a tailor but the difference is how much they are actually in their field and how talented they are…

Let us take the example of an Indian who is known by his title - 'MBA Chai-Wala'.
Had MBA Chai-Wala ever thought of 9 to 5 job or considered Chai-Wala as a profession of lower rank then he would not have been able to: -

- Open 22+ franchise of MBA Chai-Wala
- Generate 5 lakh+ per month

- Have an estimated net worth of 3+ crore at the age of 22

Let's look at some more examples internationally.
According to Forbes World's Billionaires List,
724 i.e., as many billionaires as America has.
1.8% out of every 1 million people is a billionaire, which means, out of 50 lakh people, 9 people become billionaires.
America may have done a lot of wrongs but the one thing that is done right is that it has become a land of dreams of opportunity. A land with countless success stories and inspirational people.

- Imagine starting off as a cobbler to own 5200 retail stores all over the world. That's the Bata Family, worth $1-billion

- Imagine starting off as a newspaper boy, then becoming a door-to-door salesman, then becoming a stock trader, then becoming an internationally respected billionaire. He is Warren Buffett.

- Imagine starting off as a grocery store clerk and becoming a television billionaire. That's Oprah Winfrey (Yes, she was born into poverty, the one who was molested during her childhood and became pregnant at 14; her son was born prematurely and died in infancy.)

- A cook in McDonald's to own Amazon. That's Jeff Bezos.

- A teacher to a media career, worth $6.6 Billion. He is Star Wars creator George Lucas. (By the way his dad was the owner of a stationery store)

And you are just thinking about your career in science, commerce or arts regardless of your talent and area of interest.

"**Do not study or work to impress people. Study and work for the hunger for success. Study because you are self-fish"** *-Priyanshu*

Ah! You must be feeling motivated…
Wait! Wait! Wait!
Some of you must be thinking about the products of the Indian Education System. Yes, I am talking about Sundar Pichai and Satya Nadella.
How come they are billionaires???
Boys and Girls when we talk about Sundar Pichai and Satya Nadella we should also consider the fact that they have also completed their education from outside of India. Sundar Pichai did not secure the chair of CEO just after completing IIT instead he went to Stanford University and the University of Pennsylvania to work on his skills

and this made him the CEO of Google.

The Chief Executive Officer of Microsoft, Satya Nadella too went to the University of Wisconsin Milwaukee and the University of Chicago to develop his skills and look at things more practically.

Lads and Lasses, there's nothing that separates these people's stories from your stories. Of course, centuries of colonialism by the British and changes in our education system have made us socially engineered.

This means that young Indians everywhere have been raised in a society that constantly tells them, **YOU ARE NOT GOOD ENOUGH.** WHY?

because that's what our conquerors wanted us to believe.

The English Education Act of 1835 by Thomas Babington Macaulay fulfilled the needs of the Britishers. They solely need 3 things: -

    i. **They wanted people who sit quietly at their desks and do their work.**

    ii. **They wanted people who don't ask any questions and they should not be too creative.**

    iii. **They wanted people who could communicate in English.**

Due to this, English has now become a class rather than a language in India.

In other countries like Germany, China, France, etc. There is not as much passion or obsession for English as there is in India. If your English is not good then it is termed as poor communication in India.

There is a competition of rote learning in our education system, The one who uses Rote Learning Technique gets more marks and believe me, most of the students who have scored 97% in Sanskrit are not able to speak Sanskrit properly.

Education has become the biggest emerging business in India. Instead of having a basic history, we have so many fat books of history which are meaningless. History literally teaches you how to solve problems, grasp or understand ideas by learning what happened in the past. You can learn managerial skills, leadership and what not but we are made to learn dates of war, names of famous people and what they did.

In our education system, teachers take classes with the intention of completing the syllabus and students are in a race to get high marks instead of practical learning and discovering their talents.

The United States of America Has achieved a hundred plus Nobel laureates in science. According to India's University Grants Commission, 10.7 million students were studying science, engineering/technology or computer science in 2016-17. Even since independence, the Republic of India has produced zero Nobel laureates in science.

According to the ASER report, 83% of educated Indians are not employable.
WHY?
Because a majority of the students don't really have the skills that companies want from them

because they have grown up mugging everything. Government Schools also teach English, Students do not have a good grip on grammar even after 12-12 years of studying English. They are not even able to speak English properly.

I am sure Kindergartens are way too good as compared to all your private/government schools. The techniques used there are million times better as compared to all the rote learning techniques used in your respected schools and colleges. Your Mathematics Teacher must have taught you Pythagorean triplet but has he ever told you the real-life uses of that very formula? Have they ever explained the principles to you or did they ask you to memorise them thoroughly and instil the values? We live in an environment where everyone knows the expanded form of $(a+b)2$ which is $a2+b +2ab$. Believe me or not but if you would have mug up this formula at an early stage of your childhood, no matter whether you would have known its application or not, everyone would have appreciated you and they would have seen you as a brilliant student. We live in an Educational Environment, where no one cares about the real-life usage of $(a+b)2 = a2+b2 +2ab$ but in place of 2ab, if you say 3ab, you will see 3 people laughing at you.

A 7-year-old boy learns English without even reading a book.

Why?

Because he gets that environment. A 21-year-old boy might not be able to remember formulas and spellings because he does not get that environment.

There are/is two things missing from our Education System: -

1. Education
2. System

Apologies, I missed the 3rd one that's 'Indian' because the Education System was made by the British. Thomas Babington Macaulay is the father of our education system and he just wanted to produce employees for the ongoing British Administration.

Macaulay does not give any importance to creativity.

Believe me, due to this, those students who are scoring good in the exams, the toppers, when they enter the real life, most of them lack in confidence, courage and self-esteem.

Once a real hero said - "Education is not the amount of information that you put in the human brain, it must have man making, character making & life building assimilation of ideas. Then only by means of that education can something be gained in the world."

Well, if we look back in history, our preceptors used to focus highly on the abilities of a student.
Dronacharya also taught different

things to the *Pandavas* according to their skill set. He didn't teach everyone the same thing. Again, here everyone is taught the same syllabus and the same curriculum regardless of their capabilities.
We don't have many options in our education system.

- Science is at the top
- Commerce at the middle
- Arts/Humanities at the bottom

Now, *If You keep lions, fish, snakes, elephants all in one line and tell them to climb up the tree. They will feel for the rest of their life that they are not capable of anything.*

Every 1st grader comes to school, thinking about being a pilot, singer or a zoologist someday but as the grades go higher, those ambitions fade away… The culture slowly makes them concerned to score high and secure a high rank anywhere they go. That's how a kiddo kills his/her area of talent and creativity.

Geniuses are not the ones who score maximum marks by mugging up. Also, we should not ignore the fact that the smart students do not really get a chance of leadership and responsibility. They believe in -

He scored the highest, He is the best, He is the one.

PART 4
DISCOURAGES, ROAD BLOCKS
AND REAL-LIFE STORIES

- **Ever wondered why some of your relatives always discouraged you from taking risks?**

- **From becoming a singer or a choreographer?**

- **From becoming a goalie or a cricketer or an entrepreneur?**

To understand the WHY, we have to go back in history.
Immigration began 500–600 years ago, first by the Vikings (793–1066 AD) then by the Europeans from almost every European country,

mostly from Central, Eastern and Southern Europe.

Around the 1890s, 600,000 Italians emigrated to America, and by 1920 more than 4 million had entered the United States.

Then in the last hundred years (1920-2000) Polynesians, Caribbean, African and of course Indians.

What's common about all these folks who shifted to the USA?

They were all immigrants and risk-takers.

- Who would want to risk everything and migrate to some other country?
- Who would love to say goodbye to a happy and cheerful life?

- Who would choose to risk his/her stable life and move to some other country?

They are the modern-day Americans. Every American had an ancestor who at some point decided not to play it in a safe zone and embarked on a new journey by backing themselves and backing their abilities.

Let's compare this to an average Indian mindset.

Well, we cannot theorise, but on an average most Uncles and Aunties always discourage Indian kids from: -

- **Taking risks**
- **Chasing their dream**
- **Exploring their abilities, capabilities and talent**

They don't care if you sing or You are very talented in painting or you are a good charismatic dancer, they will not let you chase your talents but Yes, they will compare you from your cousins, your neighbours or that 'Sharma ji ka beta'.

If you are born in an Indian family, most probably you will be discouraged to chase your talent until your late 20s or perhaps after your 20s. During these 20 years, you will be living in an environment which will pressurise you to get good marks, play less, study more, speak less, kill your thoughts and suggestions, listen and follow whatever Elders say, even if it is illogical.

Most of these Uncles and Aunties were born between 1940 and 1990. This was an era in Indian history which taught us to think small and in a limited manner through a socially engineered education system. So, first of all forgive them and just remember that the next time an Uncle or Aunty discourages you from chasing your dream. What they are truly saying is - "I wouldn't have been able to do this so how do you think you are going to be able to do it"

Forget Uncles and Aunties, being a part of this socially engineered education system, I have seen teachers discouraging students. I remember in 2021, as everything slowly opened up after the lockdown, so did my tuition classes. *So there we had a male teacher, who taught us Physics.* He used to praise the intelligent students and he just discouraged the students in a very bad way who were average or below average. Well, I got the advantage as I was in the category of his favourite students as physics was my favourite subject. Look, physics is actually complicated. Hilbert too said, "Physics is too hard for physicists". So, there were a few students who were not able to grasp the theories and principles. Every Saturday we used to have a test and I used to study hard to score well & maintain my rank in the tuition. There were some students who were not able to get good marks. The test paper consisted of a total of 40 marks and 20 questions. Anyone in his tuition who scored 35 or above was his favourite but those who were not able to score at least 25, He used to write their names on the whiteboard and humiliate them in the class in the worst way possible. He literally *used* sentences such as - This boy will not achieve anything in life, blah blah blah... Like I used to enjoy his class a lot but whenever I saw him demotivating my friends, killing their confidence instead of making them understand the theories, I used to feel bad. One day he taught us refraction and just after the class, he said - "If you are not able to understand this, I assure you, you will not be able to do anything in life and you are useless". He even used this sentence in the middle of his lecture. Imagine how that particular student would have felt if somehow, he/she is not able to understand that particular topic. Imagine how embarrassed that student would have felt before raising his/her hand and asking his/her doubt to him.

I still remember in fourth grade, I found a great friend, let's name him Jack. So, Jack once asked our teacher a simple maths question and she laughed and said – "isko itna easy sum v nhi aata… Yeh toh bada hokar rikshawala banega (He doesn't know such a simple question, He will definitely become an Auto Driver)" and the rest of the students laughed at him. Just imagine how humiliated Jack must have felt. This indeed broke his confidence in a very bad way. This is how we care about the mental health of our kids. Instead of explaining the solution to that kid in a very precise manner, she just demoralised that kid…

I remember when my friend Nishant told me about one of the incidents that took place in his class. He is currently in standard 9th. So, it was a day before Raksha Bandhan. There was a boy and a girl in his school who were brothers and sisters. So, during the lunch break, the girl had a packet of lays and she just took out a piece of chips and fed the boy in his mouth. A teacher saw them. Again, we know the mentality here. So, the teacher called the girl to the staffroom along with her best friend. I don't want to explain the whole conversation because it was very toxic yet offensive. A lot of heat was there but let me tell you that the teacher in front of 7+ teachers indeed used lines such as - "Go run around the aisle, naked as a punishment". This happened in a school which is very reputed within the country.

Will he/she feel really comfortable coming to school the next day? Trust me, our teachers don't give us knowledge anymore, they just tell us how to get good grades. I hardly hear my teachers saying "think about it, little things can be so interesting" but I have definitely heard my teachers saying "revise this topic thoroughly, it is a very important question and it always comes in the exam".

Trust me, I have seen hundreds of people if you do not score good in your exams, especially in that so-called "10th board exam", your parents will be the first one to demotivate you. Forget relatives, teachers and neighbours. This society is so so SO much marks oriented that they will make you feel that you are of no use. According to them, Numbers are everything, scoring good means you will have a good livelihood, scoring less means you have no future. Talent? What's that? Here, our parents actually doe

Let's take another practical example - In an Indian Engineering College, you are taught circuits and diagrams. We are basically supposed to mug up those circuits and diagrams and on the day of the exam, you are asked to draw one of the 10 circuits whereas In Western Countries such as The United Kingdom you are shown 10 circuits and then you are asked to fabricate the 11th one. There you are supposed to understand how things work from 1 to 10 and then you design the 11th one by yourself, by your own creativity and by your talent. Boys and Girls, that is the difference between the Indian Education System and Rest

of the World's Education System
and if you don't do well in this kind
of education system, do you really
think it's a good reflection of your
real smarts in life, maybe it is not.
So next time you score low marks
in your exam, do not be
demotivated by the words uttered
by your parents and relatives. Low
marks is not a sign of being dumb
in life. Mugging up and writing on
certain topics in examination and
fetching good marks is not a sign of
intelligence. What is a sign of
intelligence is knowing how to
break down complex problems,
thought process awareness, high
creativity and there are many more
factors.

Part 5
Multiple Intelligences

According to an American psychologist from Harvard University, Howard Gardner. He explained in his book, "Frames of the Mind: The Theory of Multiple Intelligences" that people do not have a set intellectual capacity, but rather many kinds of intelligences, for example a person can be musically intelligent, but terrible with numbers. He argues that traditional psychometric views of measuring intelligence are too narrow and that they can't possibly capture all the abilities and talents people possess. Gardner states that you cannot classify human beings based on one kind of intelligence. It would be incomplete to judge someone's intelligence by one or two factors alone. Instead, to help us understand ourselves better, Gardener explains the nine types of intelligence with examples.

1. *Spatial intelligence* - The ability to generate, retain, retrieve, and transform well-structured visual images. Basically, it is the ability to consider things in three dimensions. These people are generally very creative and usually have a vivid imagination and high artistic abilities. If you have a high level of Spatial intelligence, that probably means that you should chase professions such as architecture, design and map reading.

2. *Logical-Mathematical Intelligence* - The ability to think conceptually and abstractly, and the capacity to analyse problems logically, carry out mathematical operations, discern logical or numerical patterns. These People are generally excellent at maths, reasoning skills and working with numbers. The best careers you could dominate with your logical-mathematical intelligence are coding, corporate and engineering based careers. Accountant, Statistician, Computer Analyst, etc. These are some careers where you

can flourish.

3. *Musical Intelligence* - The ability to think, produce and appreciate rhythm, lyrics, pitch and timbre or appreciation of the forms of musical expressiveness. These people are generally more sensitive to sound and often pick up on noises that others would not normally be aware of. They understand music more deeply and if you fall in the category of Musical Intelligence then you can surely opt for music composer, singer, disc jockey, musician, etc.

4. *Interpersonal Intelligence* - The ability to understand and interact effectively with others. These types of people are generally good at socially understanding people well and being able to motivate people well. If you feel like you're good at these things, business is the place you should be at. Those skills apply especially in a country like India where business is based on how good your relationships are with people, how emotionally connected you are to people. More often this type of intelligence can be found in politicians, leaders,

social workers, life coaches
and psychologists.

5. *Naturalistic Intelligence* - The
ability to identify, classify and
manipulate elements of the
environment, objects, animals
or plants. These people are
generally sensitive to subtle
changes in nature and the
environment around them.
Obviously, Botanist, Biologist,
Astronomer, Geologist, etc,
are your job options.

6. *Bodily–kinaesthetic intelligence* - The ability and capacity to manipulate objects and use a variety of physical skills. These people generally have an excellent sense of timing and a great mind-body coordination. More often they use their bodies to solve problems and create something meaningful. Dancer, Physical Therapist, Sports, Army, Carpenter, Athlete are some of the jobs if you fall in this category.

7. *Linguistic Intelligence* - The ability to understand, use and learn languages and the capacity to think in words and use these words to make oneself understood. These people are generally good at putting their feelings and thoughts into words in order to make others understand them. Curator, Author, Content Writer, Journalist, etc, these kinds of jobs weren't really available and widespread say about even ten years back but in today's day and age, they pay you good money.

8. *Intrapersonal Intelligence* - The ability of a person to relate well with people, manage relationships, being aware of their own emotional states and feelings. These people are generally self-smart. Therapist, Counselor, Philosophers, Spiritual Leaders, Psychologist and writers usually have high intra-personal intelligence and you can look for these jobs.

9. *Existential Intelligence* - The ability and capacity to tackle deep questions about human existence. These people generally think more deeply. More often they are referred to as a psychological thinker. Yoga Instructor, Meditation Instructor, Public Speaker, etc can be some good job opportunities.

Lads and Lasses, you are made to believe that marks really matter and marks will decide your future because your teachers tell you so but trust me this is not actually the case, if we look a bit deep in this education system, we will come to a term which is institutionalisation. Basically, Institutionalisation is a process of developing or transforming rules and procedures that influence a set of human interactions. If you will connect this term

with your teachers you will end up with a conclusion that they are all institutionalised. Now, this is not their fault, they judge you and force you to score good just because they have spent their entire life in a school. This is one of the major reasons why they always project marks as the most important thing and why they keep telling you to score good. The Indian Education System focuses only on marks, the worst part is when teachers compare students on the basis of their marks and then give each student different priorities. Those who get *higher* marks are considered great and successful and those who get *lower* marks are considered a disgrace to this country…

Believe me, Nowadays Success is getting a government job, Rip Talent and Skills.

Even our parents have this custom called "compare numbers" with neighbours and cousins. At the end of the day, teachers care about Money, parents care about Marks and students deal with stress, tension, suicide, etc. I assure you that geniuses are only born when they give time to their interest. Those numbers are not your whole life, numbers make your early career a little easier and if you still don't believe it, tell me what is the point of writing a 300-300 pages assignment and submitting it to a teacher who doesn't even bother to flip the page. He just puts his signature on the first page. That is all.

That hurts when you put so much effort and time in a project and the examiner just throws it without seeing it.

By doing so we are just: -

- Killing the eagerness of that student
- Killing the creativity and curiosity of that student

- Killing the interest of that student in research

India does not even feature in the top 10 best education countries in the world that have the best education systems. India doesn't even feature in this list. In fact we don't even make it to the top 40. Why???
Because we mainly focus on rote learning and mugging up. Marks are given a lot of importance. We rarely focus on learning, understanding and breaking down a concept. It's all about how many marks did you get, what was your percentage and **in** which college will you get into...?

According to the Assocham Report 2017, 93% of MBA graduates are Unemployable…

1. Education is not just about getting a degree or diploma.
2. We are treating the donkey and horse in the same way.
3. Schools are not focusing on student's thinking capability and new skills. They are focused only on the syllabus and marks.
4. Does being intelligent really mean solving 30 MCQS in 50 seconds?
5. Does education really mean to mug up topics or as Albert Einstein said - "Education is not the learning the facts, but

the training of the mind to think"

6. Does that degree really mean that someone has the ability to handle the worse to the worst situation of life?

7. Everything has changed except our Education System.

8. We switched from offline to online but the basic fundamentals are still the same.

"Success and Happiness have been found to those who have lived life to the fullest and those who are in process of thinking - Log Kya Kahenge will always be at the same path" (Priyanshu)

Step out of your comfort zone,
Time has come for the Indian
children to change their mindset.
Work on the 3 keys of life: -
1.   Change the way to think and
look towards opportunities
2.   Focus more on hard work and
diligence
3.   Think Big and Take Risks

"Different people get successful by
different ways"
Start Working on your Skills,
Start Working on your Talent,
Start Working on your Creativity
and Cognitive Skills.

Because this system might not get
you ahead of your talent in the next
few years…

WHY?

- Why are the students committing suicide?
- Why is the nature of this education system so competitive that our students have to end up taking their lives?
- Why are WE creating such a situation that a student has to take such a big step?
- Why can't we remove all these rank-based systems?
- Why can't we make education FREE for all?
- Why is there so much competition to get into an educational institution?
- Why don't we have an aptitude test?

- Why The United States of America has achieved 100+ Nobel laureates in science but after Independence, the Republic of India has produced zero Nobel laureates in science.
- Why according to the ASER report, 83% of educated Indians are not employable?
- Why do they always project marks as the most important thing?
- Why do they keep telling you to score well?
- Why are they evaluating each individual in the same way?
- Why do we need to mug up things?
- Why does a 7-year-old boy learn English without even

reading a book and a 21-year-old boy might not be able to remember formulas and spellings?

- Why according to the Assocham Report 2017, 93% of MBA graduates are Unemployable…
- Is this education system really meant to make learning interactive?
- Is this education system really meant that students should have a fun-to-learn?
- Is this education system really meant to make lectures interesting, something practical or something creative?

Part 1
Marriage & Relationships

What are marriage and relationships?

I was packing up my bag for tomorrow's class. While cleaning my study table, I found an alienated piece of paper there. It was a card, a wedding card of the daughter of my father's colleague.

As far as I heard, it seemed to be a love marriage. After packing up my bag when I finally went for dinner, I heard my parents discussing things like," Kids these days, marriage is just a game to them. They choose whomever they want to, without even taking their parent's consent. Parents' decisions no longer carry any importance to them. And at last, they end up having a divorce with their so-called self-chosen partner".

Hearing these things got me into a state of deep thoughts, a state of confusion.

- What is a marriage?

- What does an ideal marriage look like?
- Am I supposed to get upset about it, or should I be happy?

What's marriage?

Well, marriage sounds like a very serious word, isn't it? Of course, it is. But are we and our preceding and succeeding generations really taking it seriously these days?

The word "Marriage" as per our Indian families , basically means not only a bonding between two people, but two whole families. They also call it a "bonding between two souls". But are these two souls supposed to be male and female-only? Can't there be both males or both females?
Well, according to most of the 90's generation Indians "NO".
Why? Because two people of the same gender can't reproduce babies. Then how will they help in

succeeding the generation of their families? And if they can't have babies then what's the purpose of their marriage?

Isn't this what most 90's people or millennials think? It's a harsh truth but, yes.
For some reason, not known till now, most of the millennials think that we, the 20's or Gen Z, don't get mature even after the age of 18. We may achieve a number of degrees, medals and trophies, we may complete a whole 18 years of education. But at the end of the day, they still won't find us mature enough to make the decisions of our own life.

Well, we have two types of marriages existing in our society, love marriage and arranged marriage.

What is the difference between love marriage and arranged marriage?

What is love marriage?

In this two people who have been acquainted with each other for a quite long time and who have been in a relationship for quite a long time finally decide to get married and live the rest of their life together as a married couple.

What is an arranged marriage?

In this type of marriage two people who might not be acquainted with each other meet and decide to get married, and their meeting is organised by their families. So basically this marriage is fixed by the individual's family and parents.

There have been a lot of debates going on about love marriage and arranged marriage.
Is it right or wrong?
Will it benefit us or ruin us?

I know I know a lot of readers might be thinking that these immature teenagers who haven't even been exposed to the real world right now, how come they'll explain to us what's right or what's wrong?

You would've probably heard of a saying, "A child notices and observes everything". And so do we. But the difference is just that others don't want to confess or discuss these things, but we do.

What does an arranged marriage actually look like?

So, basically, you're introduced to a stranger, whom you wouldn't have met in your entire life. You don't even know his/her actual character or his/her actual background. You aren't even aware of his/her intentions. You've only been introduced to him/her for a couple of months. But, just because he/she has been chosen by your parents and family, he/she definitely must be the perfect person for you. You see the irony here?

Our parents have been teaching us since our childhood that we shouldn't talk or get close to strangers. We should stay away from them and the things which they offer us, isn't it? Well, they were right. These days, our society has been spoiled so much that you can't even trust your close ones and even the people of your own family. But my friends, according to our parents even though we wouldn't have interacted with strangers in our whole life, we do have to marry them. Yes, you heard that right. We do have to marry them and spend our life with them.

Feelings? Oh, that doesn't matter.

Compatibility? Even though you won't be having that actually but for your parents and society, you do have it.

Opinions? oh, that doesn't matter because nothing can be bigger than your family's reputation in this so-called toxic society, not even your life.

Mental health? C'mon man, these are just some freakish modern concepts.

Depression and anxiety? Oh, these are just some modern excuses.

Isn't this what most millennials think?
But are these really excuses? No, they aren't.

Isn't it strange that in our society marrying a guy you probably know well is wrong but marrying a guy who is strange to you is right? And you'll be really fascinated by knowing the criteria that 90's people use for the purpose of arranging a marriage between two people.

Even though our society has been educated a lot as compared to the earlier times, still most of the people aren't able to overcome that cliché thinking of their time. A woman is still judged and chosen for marriage on the basis of her looks, her complexion (And yes, even though the man might not be that good with looks but still everyone is going to demand a fair and pale-skinned woman for their sons), her body, her cooking skills and her beauty. And in some cases on the basis of her virginity. Yes, you read that right, virginity.

Oh, but what about her profession, qualifications and designation?

C'mon man who talks about that? The criteria of qualification and designation are only valid for the man. He might not have a good character, his personality might not get liked by the woman, he might not be supportive, he might not be caring and loving, he might be a smoker, he might be a man with violent thinking and might have intentions of harassing the woman. What if he rapes her? I mean yes, why not? You definitely can't be sure of a person's character and traits by just taking a look at his/her picture and meeting him a couple of times. But still at last all that matters for most of the 90's people is "at least he earns well" as if nothing is more important than money in our lives. And while we're talking about this, how can we forget about men who become victims of mental and physical harassment?

I mean women aren't that innocent either.

What if the woman that has been chosen by a man's family comes out to be toxic?

What if she misuses his money?

What if she harasses the man's family?

You can't be sure about his/her intentions just by looking at the character that has been portrayed by his/her family. You might say that everyone is not the same. Not everyone has bad intentions. And the choices that our parents make can never go wrong.
If that's the thing, then why do every 1 in 6 women face either physical or sexual harassment at

least once in their lives including the ones who are married?
Why does every 1 in 16 men face the same?
I mean the stats can't be untrue, right?

When asked from the 90's people about why they oppose love marriage. They said," A love marriage always results in a divorce". Yes, this might be true, but did they ever think that why does it result in a "divorce", no. They assumed that just because their sons/daughters didn't marry the person of their parent's choice, that's the reason this resulted in a divorce. But is it true?
Well, according to me, the answer is, no. Why did you think the

divorce would've taken place? It might have happened that they wouldn't have found themselves compatible enough to stay together as a married couple. There might have been some disparities and differences. And probably this didn't make them comfortable enough to live together. So, they decided to have a divorce.

Now let's have a look at the couple whose marriage would have been arranged. First of all, you might be wondering why do these couples whose marriage has been arranged never file a divorce? They must be really compatible, that's what you think, right?

But is this really true?

Or is it just our assumption that as the couples in these arranged marriages are chosen by parents that's why these marriages succeed? But do these marriages actually succeed in true means? Well as far as I've seen and observed, according to me it's a big NO.
You want to know why?
Okay, so let's have a brief discussion on this in the segments written further.

Part 2
The Groundless Criteria

When I look at the couples of my own family, I wonder how good our preceding generations are with their power of adjustment, especially the women. I mean, yes after all adjusting and spending your whole life with a stranger who is 8-10 years older than you isn't an easy task though.

If you look back to the years that passed, you'll realise that marriages at those times had few very common criterias.
For the men it was:

- Being a good earner
- Being taller than the woman he's getting married to
- And definitely being 7-10 or even more years older than

the woman or the girl (girls,
between the age of 15-18)

Does that age difference seem too much? C'mon, that's too less.
People even used to have age differences of 15-20 years.
Men used to be 10 times older than women they are getting married to.
Oh, why? Because older the man, more will be his masculinity, isn't it?
But was this age factor applied to the woman too?
For finding an answer to this let's have a look at the criterias that were used for the woman:

- The woman had to be younger, teenager if possible.
- She had to have pale, white skin.

- A perfect body.
- A perfect glowing face.
- A good cook.
- She had to have an attractive face too.
- The one who could give birth to a boy (because earlier and even now too most of the people aren't aware of the scientific reason behind the formation of a male or a female foetus)
- The one with good fertility.
- She also had to be 7-10 or 15-20 years younger than her husband.
- And also smaller than her husband in height.

But why does the woman have to be younger? Is there some

scientific reason behind a young girl marrying an older man? Well, I don't know about the scientific reason, but there is definitely something psychological behind this. As the biggest aim of the Indian families earlier was to have millions of kids in their house, and so, they wanted to have a young girl marrying their son so that she could give birth to the maximum number of kids possible. Because the younger the woman, the more fertile her body is.

Oh, but can't the woman be older than the man? Is there something wrong with this? Logically, no but according to our society's cliché standards, yes.

According to our society, if you're a man who's marrying a woman who's younger than you, then you're a real man. But if being a man, you're marrying a woman who's older than you, then they'll literally call your wife as your "mom" because according to them marrying a woman who's 5-10 years older than you is like marrying someone of your mother's age. But if a girl is married to a man, 10-15 years older than her, society will compliment them and appreciate their pair.

Similarly, if you're a man whose wife or girlfriend is taller than you, then you should feel ashamed about that and either work on your height or find someone smaller than you. Because according to our Indian society, a man always has to be taller and older than the woman. Why? Because that will reflect your masculine superiority dude. That's what most of the people think, right? But is it true? No.

A perfect relationship or marriage is the one in which both the individuals show equal dominance. It shouldn't be based upon gender or age superiority. It's totally fine if you're a man whose wife is taller or older. Normalise girls being taller than the boys. Normalise women being older than men. Because love and relationships are not something that has to be based upon these physical factors.

Marriage: Unwrapping the real sides

What actually happens in a love marriage?

Two people who have been in love for quite a long time decide to finally spend the rest of their life together. They have mutual understanding. They know each other quite well. And the best thing is that none of them will have a dominance over the other. Why? Because if they know each other, they will have positive feelings towards each other and so they won't tend to cause trouble in their partner's life, probably. As they'll be knowing each other quite well, none of them will show dominance over the other. That's the reason you won't be finding many cases of dowry and harassment in the context of love marriage.

Now, what happens in an arranged marriage?

Two people who didn't really know much about each other, whose marriage has been fixed by their parents get married. Basically, most of the time parents impose their choices and decisions of marriage on their kids. Okay, I'm not saying it's bad but it isn't that good either. Remember? I told you about those cases and stats of sexual and mental harassment a few lines back. Why do you think that happens?

Well, most of the time it's about dowry and money that people are greedy for. In India, even though we say that dowry is no longer legal, in most parts of the country dowry is still taken. Not just that. Many families arrange marriages for the greed of money and lust. Women get harassed if their families are not able to spend much money on their wedding or give much dowry to the groom's family. And as we all know that even though we call our country developed in terms of thinking, still,

200

till now men are considered superior to women in terms of almost everything. And most of the time in the context of marriage also they're considered the same, especially in the 90's generation. Earlier the greedy family of the groom used to take dowry in huge amounts along with gold jewelleries and other expensive stuff and tried their best to suck all the capital that the bride's family had. And the greed didn't end here, they also used to demand highly luxurious weddings and if for some reason the bride's family wasn't able to fulfil the demands of the groom's family, then they tried their best to insult every bit of the bride's family. And these things used to result in men getting the dominance over women.

The woman had to work on the demands of her husband and his family and had to completely cut off from her own family. There was a very famous saying back then" बेटी परायी होती है" (*daughters are alienated*), which basically meant that daughters don't really belong to their parents. And all these things weren't just faced by women but also by some men who used to get married to a greedy woman.

And this thing hasn't ended completely till now. Even now these things are taking place.

Now, you'd think that if these things are being done till now then why do parents still put their children in this trap?

Aren't they aware of the things that their children face?

Well, in most of the cases the answer is, no. They aren't aware of the things that their kids face.

You'd think, Why? And why do the people facing this, don't share their experiences with their parents?

Let's understand this with a brief example that I've witnessed in real life.

Back to the year 2014. We had a new family relocate to our apartment. That was a family of six members. Also, the two kids in that family became very well acquainted with me. Everything was going on well until that night

when I and my family members
heard a loud scream coming out of
their flat. It was the painful scream
of the mother of those kids of that
family. She was being beaten by
her husband with a leather belt.
She was screaming and crying for
help, but none of the members of
that family was able to rescue her.
She was brutally beaten up by her
husband.

You might be wondering why would
anyone beat someone this way?
What would've been the matter?
You'll be really shocked to know
the reason behind this devilish
behaviour of her husband. She was
beaten up just because her child
didn't score well in his exams.

Yes, that was the only reason. She was beaten up because even though she tried her best, her son still didn't score well. And this was just a glimpse of what that woman faced. Though she was a housewife, she still had to work 24/7 to make sure that her husband didn't get angry with her. From washing dishes to washing clothes. From cooking huge amounts of meals to making sure everyone's eating well. From trying her best to teach her kids well to getting physically harassed if her kids didn't score good marks. From managing house chores to managing the whole family. And all that her husband did was, go on a 9-5 job and show his anger upon his wife, that's it. Even after going

through all of this, that lady always had a very beautiful smile on her face.
What do you think was the reason behind this smile of hers?
Wasn't she hurt?
Didn't she want to run away from there? Of course, she must have wanted to, but why didn't she?

Now for a while, put yourself in the place of the victim who is facing these things. Imagine yourself in the place of that particular girl whose parents invested lacs and crores in her wedding and tried their best to send you into a family which according to them would keep you happy. But unfortunately, the family of the man you were married to didn't come out to be as your parents thought of.

They harass you mentally as well as physically. You are fed up with the situation that you're going through. But still, would you be able to confess to your parents about the harassment that you're facing after knowing about the efforts they put into your wedding? Obviously, no. And hence because of this most of the people whose marriage has been arranged don't file **a** divorce as divorce according to our so-called developed society is a "taboo".

I hope this very true example of mine would've reflected the real beauty of arranged marriage in front of you.

Now, what's your view upon the concept of arranged marriage? Something which most of the time can make you get into a state of depression and anxiety. Something which can even result in ruining your life. Still, for most of the millennials it's good, right? Well, sometimes it is, but most of the time it's not.

I don't really mean to make you guys go against this very concept of arranged marriage. It might be good for some people and not so good for others. It totally depends upon the individual's perception. Now reading all of these things might have got you into a state of confusion or it might have even tilted you a bit more towards the

concept of love marriage. But is
love marriage actually as good as it
seems?

Part 3
Love marriage: desired by many, succeeded by a few.

We all know that nothing in this world is perfect. Everything contains flaws in some way or the other. And the same thing applies to love marriage also. Yes, yes I know I gave too much appreciation to "love marriage" in the lines which I wrote earlier. But now it's time to discuss some drawbacks of it.

Well, it's not necessary that a love marriage always has to succeed. The durability of it totally depends upon the couple involved in the same. Whether they are really compatible or they are just into a state of attraction. Whether their love is emotional or physical. Have they been acquainted for a longer period of time or has their

relationship started just a few months or years ago?
Whether they know their partner well or not. Are they intellectual enough to understand their partner's good and bad?
Will they be able to carry responsibilities together or not?
And to be very honest these are the only things that our parents are mostly concerned about. And they definitely should be, because marriage isn't a game, right?

Now, you'd think that why are these things necessary? And why are our parents concerned about these things? Well, there are many reasons behind this. So, let's have a brief discussion on the same.

We know this very well that the world isn't really a good place anymore and the people living here are also not that good either.
It might happen that the person you are deciding to spend your whole life with, by just knowing him/her for a couple of months comes out to be toxic.
It might happen that the boy/girl towards whom you've been attracted or the boy/girl who has confessed his/her feelings towards you might have some wrong intentions towards you. I mean yes, who knows? What kind of intentions and character the boy/girl you've met a few months ago carries. A survey says that in order to get married to a person you must be acquainted with

him/her for at least 2-3 years. You should be aware of every bit of him/her, the kind of family he/she belongs to, the kind of background he/she belongs to, is he/she having any criminal record and a lot more stuff. Try to figure out the person's actual character because these days for most people, faking innocence and character isn't a big deal.

But how to know if the person you've chosen is right? Well, I guess these points might help you in doing so.

- If he/she is the right person then he/she will always support you in whatever you're doing.

- He/she will stop you from getting on the wrong path.

- He/she will motivate you to reach your goals.

- He/she will make sure that you're not being distracted from your career while being with them.

- He/she will remain with you even at your tough times.

- He/she will always be there to help you.

- He/she will respect you as well as your family.

- He/she will respect your opinions as well. show a negative dominance.

- He/she will not

- He/she will not love you on the basis of your looks.

- He/she will love you on the basis of your character and personality.

- He/she will make sure that you're comfortable with them.

- He/she will have a great understanding with you.
- He/she will help you with your development.

- He/she will trust you. And you also won't hesitate to trust them.

- He/she will be there to support you as a partner as well as a best friend.

Well, there are a lot more points but let's end our discussion of these points here only.
Now, some of you might think that though we discussed some major points here, what about the main things like love, affection and care? So, let me tell you that though, for most teenagers and some adults, love might mean always talking to your partner, always holding their hands and sitting with them. Always going on dates and

hanging out with them. But trust me, the real care and love is reflected when you support your partner in pursuing his/her career and helping them in succeeding and not by wasting their time on calls and dates.

You probably know that everything in this world has a good as well as a bad side. And so is the case with these relationships too. As we've already discussed some good points of figuring out if the person you've chosen is right or wrong. Now, it's time to discuss some negative ones too.
How to figure out that the person you've chosen is not actually right for you? So for identifying that let's

have a look at some of these points written below.

- If he/she is the wrong one then he/she may start manipulating you for doing wrong things.

- He/she will promote you for going on the wrong path.

- He/she will manipulate you to go against your family.

- He/she will make sure to cut off all your bonds with your friends.

- He/she might use your body.

- He/she might disrupt your privacy and expose your personal things publicly.

- He/she will emotionally blackmail you for doing wrong things.

- He/she might use you for your money and once they're done with that, they will leave you.

- He/she might make you get into a state of depression and anxiety.

- He/she will make you get emotionally dependent on them and then make you suffer.

- He/she will pretend to take care of you but will actually damage you from inside.

- He/she will not respect you and your opinions.

- Neither he/she will respect your family.

And **at** the end, that person will leave you in a state of trauma getting out of which might take years for you.

They can harm you in many other ways. It's totally upon you, how you make decisions of choosing the right person. And these are also the things that our parents are concerned about. Why? Because these toxic people, who carry destructive mindsets are pretty good with manipulation. They'll give you fake promises. They'll talk about rubbish yet sweet things with you. They'll make you think that they truly love you more than anyone. They'll take from you some of the most important things of your life, which are time, energy, good relations with your friends and family and most importantly your self-respect. They'll make you emotionally dependent on them and then will force you to do the things you shouldn't. Such as:

- Running away from your parents.

- Completely cutting you off from the path of your goals.

- They'll force you to change.

- They'll make you go through a situation you never wanted to.

- They'll give fake promises of keeping you in the castle of diamonds and gold but at last you both will end up wandering around the streets.

- They'll make you think that you made the best choice of your life by choosing them and then by manipulating you to run with them they'll trap you also in the vicious circle they're in.

And by the time you'll realise that the choice you made wasn't as you thought it to be, it'll be too late. And yes all the pros of love marriage that I stated in the lines written earlier don't support the things that I've just mentioned above. Love marriage looks good in true means only if it is done with the consent of your parents and not by running away with your partner. It looks good when it's celebrated and not dissed.

So, how to choose someone who'll actually keep you happy?
Go with someone who is

- Focusing on his/her career and not on how you look.

- Who promotes you to study rather than going on dates.

- Who makes you aware about the realities rather than faking fantasies.

I know, I know all these things might sound nerdy but trust me, spending hours with your partner unnecessarily won't give you your dream house.

Part 4
LGBTQ

LGBTQ: stop suppressing, start supporting

Till now we already had much discussion about marriages and relationships. But we discussed this only in the context of a man and a woman. We all know that a third community also exists in our society. As educated individuals of this country, almost all of us are very well aware of the LGBTQ community. Yes, the community which according to me might take decades to get acceptance from a country like India. First of all, let's discuss the meaning of "LGBTQ". What is LGBTQ? Firstly, let's start with its full form.

- L: lesbian; in this two females are emotionally and sexually attracted towards each other.
- G: Gay; in this two males are emotionally and sexually attracted towards each other.

- B: Bisexual; in this an individual, either male or female is attracted emotionally and sexually towards both the genders male as well as female.

- T: Transgender; an individual whose gender identity differs from the sex the person had or was identified as having at birth especially.

- Q: Questioning; someone who's still exploring his/her gender identity.

Now, after knowing about the proper meaning of "LGBTQ" you'd realise how interesting this community is, isn't it? Yes, surely it is but still for most people especially Indians, this subject of LGBTQ is taboo. And this isn't the case only with the 90's people. Even some people of our generation, 20s too, consider it the same. Why? Because according to most Indians, belonging to this community is a sin. In a typical Indian family, people become so blinded by the dark clouds of their mythological thinking about this community that they don't even care if some kid belonging to their family belongs to the community of LGBTQ.

They won't care if you belong to their family, once you've been identified as a transgender, gay, lesbian or bisexual they'll not think twice before throwing you out of their house. Yes, this might sound a bit untrue but this is the actual truth. If you're a gay or a lesbian who isn't interested in marrying a person of the opposite gender and even though you confess this to your parents, still they'll force you to go with their decision of marrying the person of opposite gender. Oh, but parents always think about the welfare and happiness of their children, right? Yes, they do but not in this context. Their concerns about your welfare and happiness end at the point society comes in.

Yes, "Society", something which has been sucking the blood of most of us for centuries. You'll make a single mistake and this so-called society will start judging you, even if they don't know anything about you. You might be an independent individual and a good earner but if you're getting into something like the LGBTQ community, they'll start dissing you and your family. You might be a good individual but if you're not coping with the conservative and destructive thinking of the society then according to most of the 90s people, you don't deserve to exist here. You'll be shocked to know that though parents always tend to be with you, if at some point you do something that goes against the mindset of our existing society, then there's a 95% chance that they'll also start treating you the way society does. Sounds strange but it's true.

So, let's come back to the topic about which we were discussing, the mindset of people towards LGBTQ. Most of the people from our Indian society, who are illiterate with their thinking, consider this community a sin without even knowing the actual scientific reason behind their existence. Oh, science? C'mon man these things have no relations with your science. It's a curse given by God, most of the Indians think the same, right? But we, being well-educated citizens of our country, should be aware of the actual reasons behind this and try our best to put down all the myths about this very community.

Why don't people accept the ones who belong to this community?

There are numerous reasons behind this but let's focus on the main one. According to most Indians, getting engaged with an individual of the same gender will hurt the sentiments of our Almighty God. Is it true? No. Any of the holy books of any religion or caste never stated that the marriage of two individuals of the same gender is a sin. It's just the foolish and superstitious mentality of the people which makes them have

these kinds of opinions and
thoughts.

Aren't people belonging to the
community of LGBTQ also
humans?
Don't they belong to the same
planet where we also live?
Yes, they do, and thus they should
have liberty and freedom in their
lives as per their desire to marry
the person they want and not what
society suggests. But will our
society understand this and accept
this community and these
relationships? No, not really.
They'll bully the people who are
involved in the same and try their
best to kill them with the painful
wounds of their harsh words. Due
to these factors, LGBTs are not

able to live a comfortable and happy life.

- They're always suppressed and fearing about various things.

- They're afraid to have relationships.

- They're afraid to reveal their relationships in front of society.

Some surveys have stated that LGBT youths suffer a lot from panic attacks, depression and anxiety. And now this won't make you get into a state of shock that why LGBTs commit suicide. The Suicide Prevention Resource

Center gave an estimation that between 5 and 10% of LGBT youth, depending on their age and sex groups, have attempted suicide at a rate of 1.5-3 times higher than heterosexual youth or the youth who doesn't belong to this community. [source: Wikipedia]

Why do you think these people commit suicide? Let's have a look at some of the reasons behind this.

- High prevalence of bullying by classmates in school, college and other places.

- They are pressured by family and society to have normal relationships (relationships with the opposite gender) which are acceptable by them and get married.

- They lack emotional support when things don't go well in their relationships.

- Sometimes they feel that the relationship cannot reach its actual conclusion.

- They fear losing their partner because of family pressure to get married.

- They are scared about not finding love again, as fewer LGBT people are present in the society currently.

- They are always under the pressure of keeping their relationship hidden as the society won't accept them.

When will we stop seeing LGBTs and their relationships with the eyes of hatred?
When will we accept them and let them be as they want to be?
When will we start respecting their gender identity?

It's time to put a full stop to all the stereotype thinking of ours about this community and the kind of relationships they hold. It's time to support them, not suppress them.

Part 5
Cohabitation

Cohabitation: a solution to the despairing endings

We talked about all these things i.e., love marriage, arranged marriage and LGBTs marriage. We came to know about the kind of chaos that is present in all these marriages. Every kind of marriage or relationship contains drawbacks or flaws in some way or the other. But we all know that every problem existing in this world does have solutions. You just need to explore it.

I was sitting on my chair taking a mild sunbath with the ray of sunlight coming in my room, holding a pen and wondering that though I wrote about the pros and cons about some types of relationships, isn't there any other way of avoiding this chaos other than having a divorce or a break-up?

I was tired of thinking and finding a solution to this. As I was about to close my diary, leaving the discussions about which I wrote in the middle. I heard the doorbell ringing. My mother opened the door, and our new neighbours were standing there. They were a couple in a "live-in relationship", who recently shifted to our apartment and were living on the 15th floor. They came to us to say "hello" and introduce themselves. They seemed to be belonging to a good family. My mother invited them for

dinner too. After seeing and observing them for quite a while, I finally got the solution to the things that were going on in my mind. The solution to the chaos that takes place in marriages and relationships.
Live-in relationships, a solution to all the misunderstandings that take place in marriages, to be specific, in love marriages.

What is a live-in relationship or cohabitation?

A cohabitation or live-in relationship is an arrangement where two individuals are not married but live together. They can be a male and a female, both females or both males. Once again, this topic of "live-in relationship" is a taboo subject in India. I mean what's not a taboo in India? Anyways, let's get back to our discussion.

So, even though our law says that cohabitation is permissible and there's nothing unlawful in this. Still, for most Indians, especially 90s people or millennials, it's illegal. It's because according to them living with a person whom you're in a relationship with is a crime. Once again, this is also something not accepted by our so-called society. And if you are indulged in something like that, they won't leave a single chance to insult you and your parents. Oh yes, our parents, how can we forget them? Even they won't let you live peacefully if you want to get indulged in a live-in relationship.

Our court has already given clarity by stating that live-in relationships are not illegal or an offence in the eyes of law, it is considered immoral in the eyes of the conservative Indian society, the society which can never bear the happiness and freedom of other people. A society that can develop only in terms of economy and not in terms of thinking.
The court also said that a live-in relationship is a right to life and personal liberty and hence it is not illegal. Oh, but c'mon did any spiritual book ever stated anything

about cohabitation? No. Has any holy or superstitious person ever called this concept good? No. Then how come our society will accept this? Well, there is no proper answer to this question.

We discussed so much about the concept of cohabitation or live-in relationship but didn't really discuss the main points.

- Is it good or bad?

- Should we get into this or not?

- What are its advantages and disadvantages?

So, in order to get a clear answer to all these questions mentioned above, let's have a discussion and come to a conclusion about this topic.

Why should we have live-in relationships? Is it advantageous?

When you're in a relationship with someone, the maximum you'd know about that person might be his/her character, family background, thinking, behaviour, traits and maybe some of his/her likes and dislikes. But are you completely aware of your partner's habits and routines? Your partner's hygiene? In some cases yes, but in most of the cases no.

What if you are a hygienic person but the one you are about to get married to isn't the same. How will you come to know about this? what if he/she just pretends to be well-maintained but actually isn't and when you get married, you come to know about this and you dislike this thing about the particular person you're married to.

- What if this thing frustrates you?

- What if the person you are getting married with doesn't live the way you like to or he/she doesn't manage the things the way you like to?

What if he/she doesn't have the proper etiquette for eating?

- What if he/she keeps his/her room messy? What if he/she doesn't know how to manage his/her work?

- What if he/she doesn't know how to properly share a bed while sleeping?

I mean yes, these things might sound a bit weird but these things are definitely important in order to lead a comfortable life with your partner. Many of you might also say that marriage and relationships are based on compromises. But for compromising too, you need some space and time in order to adjust properly.

This may sound awkward but, in many cases, the divorces even take place because of these reasons, yes, the reasons which include your partner not living in a proper way. Now suppose you are a hygienic boy or a girl who has been married to his/her partner after two to three years of relationship, just a relationship, not a cohabitation and when you get married, after 2 to 3 days you realise that when your partner is cooking in the kitchen he/she is not actually keeping the kitchen clean. I don't really mean to make your partner work like a slave in the kitchen, but there is some sort of hygiene that has to be maintained, isn't it?

You are a very disciplined person who loves to keep everything in a well managed way, but your partner doesn't know how to do the same. He/she throws away his/her clothes on the bed carelessly and doesn't even know how to organise and manage a wardrobe. He/she doesn't know how to keep his/her things properly. What if he/she carelessly keeps a wet towel on the bed and you don't like it? What if you are a very well-maintained person, but your partner isn't and you don't like that? Will not that frustrate you? Yes, that definitely will. In order to live a happy and comfortable life with your partner and to know how to adjust yourself according to them, you need to be very well aware of every bit of him/her.

- How does he/she eat? What kind of lifestyle does he/she have?

- Is he/she hygienic?

- Is he/she a careless or a careful person?

- How does he/she manage his/her things?

- Does he/she know a proper way to maintain a house?

Yes, I know, these things sound a bit like old age kind of thinking to some modern people, but to be honest these things are definitely necessary in order to live properly. And all these things are not just applied to women but also to men. Would you be able to know about all of this just by going on some dates and having long conversations on calls? Well, I don't think so. What's your opinion on this? Well, according to me, in order to be very well aware of all of these things, which is actually really very important in contemplation to live comfortably and happily and avoid things like divorce and breakups. The best solution that has been introduced to us is cohabitation or live-in relationship. Cohabitation or live-in relationship as it states basically means living with your partner whom you are in a relationship with without getting married. By being in a live-in relationship you would be able to know each and everything which your partner does. From eating to bathing, from keeping the wardrobe clean to how does your partner keep the house.

All these things are necessary in order to avoid chaos later on. But is cohabitation allowed to only those people who are about to get married in the future? No, not really. It's also applicable to the people who want to live with their partner but not under the label of marriage.

This might not seem a proper way of living to most of the Indians, but we should learn to respect the freedom and liberty of others and how they want to live.

Learn to accept the diversity: inter-caste and inter-religion marriages

It was 10 p.m. at night. I was writing my journal and was about to go to bed when I suddenly found a newspaper lying on the floor. I picked it up. There was something written in bold letters, it was a highlighted article of that newspaper that stated the story of a couple who committed suicide because their families weren't supporting them for their marriage.

Yes, now it's time to discuss one of the biggest problems of our Indian society. The problem that most couples who want to have a love marriage face. Why do you think the couple about whom it was written in the newspaper committed suicide? Maybe because their parents didn't accept them or probably because of the very toxic society of ours.

- Why did their parents not accept them?

- What could be the reason behind their disagreement?

- Weren't those couples human beings?

- They definitely were. Then why did their parents oppose them?

- Why did they go against them?

These questions were running in my head too until I read the whole article about that suicide case. And as expected, the reason behind the death of that couple was the unacceptance of their marriage by their parents and society because of caste and religious differences.

Yes, they committed suicide because of the pressure of our very own Indian society, which doesn't accept inter-caste or inter-religion marriages.

But why? Because according to their cheap thinking and opinions, marrying or coming in contact with someone who belongs to another caste is a sin and it will make you toxic and unclean or typically said, अशुद्ध (*ashuddh*).

I have got a question for all the readers out there. Do you all find any literal logic behind this concept? Well to me it's a big No. Don't the people who belong to other castes or religions have blood in their veins or is there any sort of chemical running through their bodies?

Don't they look like humans?

Or is there any sort of religious symbol imprinted on their bodies?

I don't know about you all but a normal human being like me has never noticed either of the things mentioned above or any other strange thing that differentiates people physically on the basis of their religion or caste. And to be very honest, nothing in this world exists that would differentiate people in this context.

Then why does our society differentiate?

So, by not extending the discussion much further, let's come to the main point. What do you think our Indian society loves the most? Yes, yes I know the thing which they love the most is suppressing people, spreading rumours, judging and giving their toxic illogical opinions. But here we're going to talk about their ultimate pleasure, the pleasure of creating big families by producing hundreds of babies, without even thinking about the health of the female who's producing them or knowing if they'll be able to handle the expense of that large family which they're creating.

And you'll be shocked to know that the reason for our society getting against this concept of inter-caste and inter-religious marriage has some relations with creating big families too.

The biggest aim of our conservative Indian society is to keep on succeeding the generations of their families. That's the reason why in many parts of India, even now married women with low fertility are abandoned. Yes, the only reason behind abandoning them is their low fertility rate or if they're not able to reproduce a boy.

Now, let's correlate this with the concept of opposition to inter-caste and inter-religious marriage with an example.

Suppose a Hindu boy gets married to a Christian girl. They had a baby who was perfectly fine physically as well as mentally. But still, the boy's and the girl's parents didn't accept the baby which had the genes of their very own son and daughter.

What could be the reason behind this?

Why didn't the family accept the baby as a part of their succeeding generation?

The reason is that the new born baby who was an outcome of a Hindu boy and a Christian girl, didn't have the genes of a particular religion. The baby inherited the genes of both Christianity as well as Hinduism and thus was considered impure and not a part of the succeeding generation of their family.

And this example doesn't only imply on Christians or Hindus. It's implied to every caste and religion existing in India. From Hindus to Punjabis to Muslims to Christians and many other religions face the same. Just because the people of different castes and religions worship different Gods, people think marrying them is a sin. Even couples who belong to the same religion but different castes had to face the same. If you're someone who belongs to the upper caste of a religion and wants to marry a person who belongs to the lower one, according to the groundless standards set by our society, (Don't *take these examples in context of the promotion of caste or religious discrimination, we're just writing this on the basis of society's point of view. All the caste and religions are equal in our point of view.)* you still have to struggle a lot. And even though you get married to that person with your parent's consent, society might still consider you the black sheep of your family.

When will our society get independent with its irrational thinking?

It's the bitter truth that flaws in our Indian society are literally unending in most of the context. They won't let you live peacefully if you don't match their conservative standards. Because they can't see you shining or being independent.

You might be getting suppressed in your married life but you can't speak because of the society's pressure. You don't want to have babies but you have to produce them or else society will have its own assumptions towards you and your partner. You want to live in cohabitation but you can't because

267

society will start spitting on your character.

You can't publicly walk with a person of the opposite gender because society doesn't accept that.

- To any of the readers who've been in an arranged marriage or have seen a couple being in an arranged marriage, haven't you guys ever witnessed the harsh truths of violence and dominance even once in your life, which are written in this book?

- What do you think is actually wrong with our society?

- Why can't they support LGBTs?

- Why can't they raise their standards?

- Why can't they start thinking practically?

- When will they start giving intellectual opinions?

- When will they become well educated?

- When will they start releasing about the mistakes they make?

- When will they stop mentally torturing us?

- When will they stop imposing their opinions on us?

- When will our society mature?

- When will they start supporting love marriages?
- When will they start realising about the real side of arranged as well as love marriages?

- When will they start supporting LGBTQs?

- When will they start supporting relationships?

- When will they stop considering cohabitation as taboo?

- When will our country become fully independent in the context of thinking?

EPILOGUE

*DON'T LET YOUR FEAR OF FAILURE STOP
YOU FROM REALIZING YOUR DREAMS.*

5th February 2022, 9:00pm
As Anushka and Priyanshu together made a
plan to write and asked me if I was in.
5 minutes later I wrote back that this is the best
idea I've ever heard.
We all were scared and shivering, thought we
might have decided to do something that is not
possible for us to write.
We questioned each other several times,
Aren't we too young to write?
What have we faced in this life?
What sort of experience do we have for this?
One thing shouted in our minds," we are doing
something that might hurt people,
We are doing something that might be wrong."
The fact that we are making a terrible plan and
it might fail, forced us quite a few times to give
up writing and stay mum like most people. But,
we decided to do it without fearing the
consequences. As, honesty that we have
inside us will give us courage to fight all the
challenges.

In the last three years we have witnessed an
exciting though exhausting journey. We have
seen happiness that comes with a lot of
struggles. We might not have experience, we
might not have the best qualifications. But, one
thing that we have inside us is to bring a

change. A change not just in ourselves, but a change in the way how society works.

This book is a combination of three different point-of-view on subjects that are different from each other. Yet, being very similar to each other. We tried to shape the subject as per our knowledge and experience about it. It is not written with the purpose of harming anyone's interest, or feelings.
Growing up we see all this happening around us, we see people putting pressure on each other for the sake of their own pleasure.
Forcing each other according to society's mind, thinking, lifestyle, and various other factors.
But, it's time we start raising questions. Not just to ourselves, but to everyone around us.
Start calling out everyone, for all the discomforts and pressure we have because of them.
"Look at questions as key rings.
 Questions unlock doors.
The bigger key ring and the more keys you have, the more doors you can unlock."

A NOTE ON THE AUTHOR

Muskan, Priyanshu & Anushka are the students of standard 10th, They participated and organised lots of debates and raised voices against injustice. Muskan won a few inter-school debate competitions. Priyanshu is into MUNs, he is honoured by the medal of distinction in International General Knowledge Competition and made it to the top 1% in the Assessment of Scholastic Skills. Anushka is a National Rank Holder and she too won lots of high commendation in MUNs.

In standard 8th, they started a campaign, under which they helped 27 poor families with their own savings. In standard 9th, they helped 77 poor and needy students by making them aware of the need & necessity of education and distributed study kits which consisted of a pencil box, eraser, pen and all the accessories along with a cap and notepad. Currently they are planning to launch a free initiative to help people, who are dealing with anxiety & depression via online mode.

www.ingramcontent.com/pod-product-compliance
Lightning Source LLC
Chambersburg PA
CBHW020904160726
47993CB00005B/1814